NEW DELHI DOWN THE DECADES

NEW DELHI DOWN THE DECADES

A Behind-the-lens View of the City

Dhruva N. Chaudhuri

NIYOGI BOOKS

Published by

NIYOGI BOOKS

D-78, Okhla Industrial Area, Phase-I
New Delhi-110 020, INDIA
Tel: 91-11-26816301, 49327000
Fax: 91-11-26810483, 26813830
email: niyogibooks@gmail.com
website: www.niyogibooksindia.com

Design: Write Media

ISBN: 978-93-81523-86-5
Year of Publication: 2013

Printed at: Niyogi Offset Pvt. Ltd., New Delhi, India

Contents

King George V and Queen Mary holding court, Delhi Durbar, 1911.

Foreword

In Nirad Chaudhuri's *Thy Hand, Great Anarch!* we read a Calcutta denizen's impressions of the grandeur and the vastnesses of a very young New Delhi, its trees only a few feet high, its bungalows deserted for half the year. It has been left to one of his sons, the talented photographer Dhruva, to take the story further, to describe how the new capital coped with the flood of immigrants in 1947-48, and changed from being the sparsely-populated, slow-moving five-month capital of British India, into the all-weather capital of India.

Dhruva Chaudhuri needs no introduction—he, with Maheshwar Dayal, Imdad Sabri, Akhilesh Mittal and R.V. Smith, constitutes that little group that has done a service to Delhi's inhabitants by interpreting their city. He has an advantage over the others in that he wields not only a pen, but a camera. In the last few years many illustrated books have been published on the Durbar of 1911 and on the construction of the monumental buildings of New Delhi. But this book goes well beyond the other—here are selections from a priceless archive of half-a-century, photographs with a quality of beauty because of the play of light and shade, and a quality of charm because of the author's sense of irony and quirky sense of humour.

His razor-sharp memory makes Dhruva Chaudhuri an archive in himself. After recounting the oft-told tale of the choice of architects and the arguments about site and style, he becomes part of the story. From 1952 (the date of the cover photograph) we embark on a leisurely journey through half-a-century. It takes a lot of imagination today to visualise young Dhruva travelling by bullock cart from Kashmiri Gate to Teen Murti to collect the furniture being sold by a British civil servant; on the journey home he sits under the dining table to escape the mid-day heat! He has conversations with Walter George, who had been part of Lutyens' team and stayed on to design institutional buildings in the modern style which he thought totally appropriate for the capital of India. In those glorious days when the word 'security' was not heard, and the Delhi Police were not with us or for us always, Dhruva and his camera wandered around without let or hindrance, recording the Prime Minister's House, Chanakyapuri, and Broadcasting House (the imposing new avatar of the radio station in the Civil Lines where his father had worked). He photographs the undulating area around Purana Qila which was being redesigned into Sundar Nagar and the Zoo, and the construction of Krishi Bhavan and Udyog Bhavan, shabby cousins to Baker's Secretariat buildings. He is struck by the architecture of the churches and gurdwaras in New Delhi, and equally by the monuments of Kotla Mubarakpur before it was engulfed by South Extension One. When Delhi began to go vertical, he saw opportunity— he could now capture the aerial views which earlier had required a low-flying aeroplane.

With their unfailing knack for bad timing, the British had built an expensive imperial capital precisely in those years when everyone could see that the days of the empire were numbered. But, as Mahesh Buch pointed out, the imperial city was also a democratic one. It could be comfortably navigated by a pedestrian, even after the few dozen cars in the city had multiplied to tens of thousands. And leading the pedestrians is Dhruva Chaudhuri, camera slung round his neck, urging us to make time to "stand and stare". So switch on the lamp, settle down in your favourite chair, and read on...

Narayani Gupta
December 2012, New Delhi

First Look

New Delhi, the capital city of India, has just completed hundred years since it was founded on 12 December 2011 and I am standing at the very spot inside Coronation Park where King-Emperor George V declared that the capital of British India would henceforth be the historic city of Delhi instead of Calcutta (now Kolkata). Looking at the bleak and dismal landscape, it is hard to imagine what a grand and colourful spectacle it was hundred years ago, on the day of the Delhi Durbar in 1911, with King George V and Queen Mary holding court with their subjects from British India and the princes of the Indian States.

Plaque on Coronation Pillar announcing the coronation of King George V at Delhi Durbar, 12 December 1911.

New Delhi, or rather Lutyens' Delhi as it is now known, was still young—just over ten years of age—when, after coming to Delhi with my parents and brothers, I had my first look at the capital city of India in June 1942. So it is all but natural for some of us who have seen the city grow in the last seven decades, from a quiet garden city into a giant metropolis, to remember how beautiful and impressive New Delhi looked as we walked, rode a bullock cart, or viewed it from an aeroplane.

As for me, the story of Imperial Delhi began long ago on a dark and smoke-laden winter evening of Calcutta in January 1938. As a youngster about to touch five, I was recovering from a serious attack of diphtheria and an early antibiotic called Prontocil had made me restless. To keep me from throwing tantrums, my maternal grandmother, Sureshnandini Devi, decided to read out a story about the Delhi Durbar of 1911, where King George V, the first British monarch to visit India, had announced the shifting of the capital of India to Delhi. That particular story of Delhi Durbar in a Bengali magazine was actually a literal translation of a report from *The Imperial Visit to India 1911*, as quoted by R.E. Frykenberg in *The Coronation Durbar* of 1911. It read: "After the final invocation of God Save

Coronation Pillar, where King George V declared Delhi as the capital of British India.

Statue of King George V, now located at the Coronation Park, Delhi.

the King-Emperor, and trumpets sounding the final fanfare, King George V suddenly got up from his seat and after taking a scroll from the Governor General, Lord Hardinge, began to read aloud: 'We are pleased to announce to our people that on the advice of our ministers, we have decided upon the transfer of the Seat of the Government of India from Calcutta to the ancient Capital of Delhi'."

This historic statement was such a well-guarded secret, orchestrated mainly by Lord Hardinge, that even Queen Mary, the Empress, was taken by surprise. The foundation stone was ordered and hurriedly prepared only after this announcement and laid by King George V on 15 December

1911. The original foundation stone was moved to its present location between the two Secretariat blocks after Raisina Hill was chosen as the final place for the three main buildings of the Government of India. According to the renowned author Khushwant Singh, his father Sir Sobha Singh, then a young man, moved the foundation stone all the way from its original site near the Flagstaff Tower on the western side of Northern Ridge of Delhi in a bullock cart while he himself walked all through the night till the cart reached its destination.

As chance would have it, on a cold December morning of 1942, my father Nirad C. Chaudhuri, still an 'Unknown Indian', decided to go to the Coronation Park for his morning walk, and as per his usual habit took me and my brother Kirti, both less than ten, in tow. As we walked all the three miles to the Coronation Pillar, Father went on to describe how King George V and Queen Mary had arrived on a special train from Bombay (now Mumbai) on 7 December 1911 and were received by Lord Hardinge, the Viceroy, and other dignitaries such as the members of his Executive Council and heads of Princely States. After alighting from the royal train at a special station inside the Salimgarh Fort, next to the Red Fort, the Emperor and the Queen were taken in a grand procession through the royal palaces inside the Red Fort and past Jama Masjid, to the royal encampment across the Ridge to the site, where later the old Viceregal Lodge was built and is now the Delhi University Vice-Chancellor's office.

A few weeks before our excursion to the Coronation Pillar we had walked to Kotla Firoz Shah, located just outside the Delhi Gate of the old city and had observed an equestrian statue of the late King Edward VII inside a park in front of Jama Masjid. Right from my young days I found this statue, the only equestrian one in Delhi, to be rather exciting and managed to take a good photograph of it in the early fifties of the last century. A few years later I came across an old copy of the *Imperial Gazette* printed in Calcutta, which mentioned that this particular memorial to King Edward VII was sculptured by Sir Thomas Brock and had cost about rupees five lakhs, raised by public subscription. On 8 December 1911, King George V had unveiled this statue at an elaborately orchestrated ceremony

Statue of King Edward VII, unveiled by George V, 8 December 1911.

and a good section of the Emperor's procession had passed through Mori Gate, almost next to our house on Nicholson Road.

On our return from the Coronation Park, Father decided to walk through the old cantonment area, which till the late forties was dotted with abandoned pillboxes and magazine chambers that were more than a century old. Roads, too, had names such as Probyn Road, Lancer's Lane

Viceregal Lodge, now Delhi University.

and Cavalry Lines. This area of Civil Lines, right next to the Northern Ridge, had already become the campus of the University of Delhi. The palatial bungalow here was once the temporary Viceregal Lodge. In 1942 it was the Vice-Chancellor's office with the huge ballroom turned into the main university library. It was in this library, while studying for a Science degree in 1952, that I did some of my preliminary work for three illustrated articles on New Delhi. It was also from certain publications in this library that I came to know that, apart from the Viceroy's House, a temporary Secretariat building had to come up for the government to function in Delhi instead of Calcutta. E. Montague Thomas was the architect who built the Old Secretariat in Civil Lines in a hurry. That twin-towered building served as the official venue of the Government of India for almost twenty years before moving on to New Delhi. It is perhaps ironic to observe that the same Old Secretariat building is still going strong as the Legislative Assembly of the Delhi State Government.

Designing Delhi

"New Delhi has an architectural history of great human, political and artistic interest. But very little attention is paid to it." That is how I began my first article of the series, *The Acropolis of Delhi*, published nearly sixty years ago in August 1953. One of the reasons for this lack of interest in the architecture of New Delhi could have been because of the existence of the older Indo-Islamic monuments, I argued, and then went on to mention that there was perhaps also a deeper psychological factor. Viceroy Hardinge and King George V were in favour of an Indian style of architecture, whatever that may signify, for all important buildings such as the Viceroy's House and the Secretariats. On the other hand, decision-makers such as the two principal architects, Sir Edwin Landseer Lutyens and Sir Herbert Baker, went overboard to create an imperial style of architecture in all the three important buildings on Raisina Hill. Baker, overwhelmed with the prospect of working with Lutyens, wrote: "The new capital of India must not be Indian, nor English, nor Roman, but it must be *Imperial*."

The renowned architect Sir Edwin Landseer Lutyens.

Lutyens' name was first recommended as the third member of the Delhi Town Planning Committee by Reginald Blomfield, then the President of the Institute of British Architects. The two other members of this group were John Brodie and Captain George Swinton. This committee found that the site for the new capital north of Civil Lines, in and around the site of the

Coronation Durbar, was far from suitable. After considerable exploration, usually on an elephant, the present location of New Delhi—around Raisina Hill, south of the old city of Shahjahanabad—was found.

After choosing the location, the construction work on New Delhi was held up due to World War I. It was resumed with full force in 1919 and then onward Lutyens had, apart from Baker, a team of able architects—Robert Tor Russell, Arthur Gordon Shoosmith, Henry A. Medd and Walter Sykes George—who made Delhi his home till his last days in 1962. Horticulturists such as Grierson and W.R. Mustoe were mainly responsible for making New Delhi a garden city.

Walter George, whom I had the privilege of knowing in the fifties of the last century, mentioned in a seminar that the Government of India had no idea initially about how the new capital of India should be designed. According to this veteran architect, what emerged was more a road plan than a proper town plan. The site chosen south of the old city of Delhi was completely rocky and barren, also dotted with old villages along with mosques and tombs in ruins. The change brought about by Lutyens to this unpromising site was truly the work of a visionary. But, in order to find out what Lutyens thought while planning New Delhi, we have to read an interesting interview between Edwin Lutyens and Sir Sobha Singh, the principal contractor of New Delhi buildings (I am grateful to my esteemed friend, who was also once my student, Professor Malay Chatterjee from the School of Planning and Architecture, New Delhi, who allowed me to quote this interview from one of his reports on New Delhi). Professor Chatterjee came across a transcript of this interview in the 'Oral History' section of the Nehru Museum Library. According to Lutyens, the entire street planning of New Delhi—with its generous right-of-way, roundabouts and tree plantation—was done with a view to encourage future high-density development. The initial low-density bungalow and hutment zones, as elaborated by Lutyens, were only a temporary phase appropriate for the initial stage of urban development. He even went on to predict that, in the future, six-storey buildings would be a common feature in many of the New Delhi streets like in some of the capital cities of Europe, including London.

Lutyens and other architects spent at least three to five months in Delhi every year, mostly during the winter season. After a low-key ceremony held on 13 February 1931 where Lord Irwin, Governor General of India, inaugurated New Delhi, Lutyens walked out of one of the main portals of the Viceroy's House. It was perhaps an irony of fate that within a week of New Delhi's inauguration, Mahatma Gandhi, a severe critic of New Delhi, himself entered the Viceroy's House through the same doors to sign the Gandhi-Irwin pact.

The Secretariat, with a view of the Jaipur Column on Raisina Hill.

Rashtrapati Bhavan, east front with Jaipur Column.

Then, about a year after India's Independence in 1947, the grand portals of the Governor General's house were open to all including me, still a teenager. The main Durbar Hall along with some other rooms and passages were thrown open to exhibit the national treasures of India's art and sculpture. C. Rajagopalachari, as the first Indian Governor General, along with Pandit Jawaharlal Nehru, the first Prime Minister of India, took the initiative to arrange an exhibition of historical art objects as a precursor to the National Museum of Indian Art. For me it was not only a grand opportunity to see some of the finest examples of Indian art, but to also get a close-up view of the grandeur of Lutyens' architecture. Though hard to believe today, no questions were asked about my camera even when used with a tripod.

I did take some photographs of the Governor General's house, both interiors as well as the outside, yet severe restraints of money, equipment and also my lack of experience prevented me from doing an adequate job of photographing Lutyens' magnum opus. Finally, just after New Delhi had completed twenty years of its inauguration, I got an opportunity to work on three illustrated articles on New Delhi buildings, encouraged by P.W.J. Crosland, the magazine editor of a leading English newspaper that was published from New Delhi and Kolkata. The three large volumes on Lutyens' work by A.S.G. Butler, available in the Central Secretariat library, which I could access through the kindness of the late O.K. Ghosh, a senior official at that time, were really useful. So was the biography by Christopher Hussey with inputs from Mary and Robert Lutyens. And, of course, there were constant intellectual and factual hammerings from my illustrious father.

Magnificent Vision

There was another school of thought, equally English, which held different views. These were vigorously expressed by Mrs Coates, a novelist and also a newspaper correspondent. She did not see the necessity of an ambitious imperial city, but was for a small city on the North Ridge that would be suitable for ceremonial purposes alone. She told Lutyens that twenty-five years ahead was all that the Government needed to contemplate for. Anything further was in the laps of the gods. Lutyens reported that Mrs Coates had no arguments or facts to substantiate her surmise. But in the end it was her estimate, not Baker's or Lutyens', which proved more correct. For, with the transfer of power to those who fought the imperial concept, all interest in the history of New Delhi had waned till recent years.

The Indian opinion was severely critical of the expenditure on New Delhi and this criticism was a nightmare to successive Viceroys and Finance Members, who were always scaling down the plans and estimates of Lutyens' New Delhi. The irritated architect prompted his friend Sir Walter Raleigh to write the following lines aimed at Sir William Meyer, the Finance Member of the Viceroy's Executive Council:

> "I sing of a city uprising
> Like the newest of Aphrodites
> From a jungle of tombs and temples
> A City of Dreadful Knights..."

On another occasion, in order to overcome the objections of Mahatma Gandhi who was deploring the expenditure on architectural piles as

Secretariat, South Block—the imposing building seen through grills.

a waste of money, Lutyens tried to get Pandit Motilal Nehru, the Prime Minister's father, interested in his project. He told Motilal Nehru that it was all Indian work and much more worth doing than spinning, adding that India once led in the fine arts, but was now deplorably behind. Motilal Nehru was wearing a black sherwani and churidar pyjamas. Lutyens drew buttons on the legs of the pyjamas and said that Motilal was now looking exactly like an English bishop and that would be all that he was fit for if he did not help India in its material needs.

We have no evidence that Motilal Nehru was able to do anything for Lutyens. The estimates on both the Secretariat and Viceroy's House were cut down. This explains the neglect of the architectural history of New Delhi, but does not justify it. Even when the political concept behind the building of a city comes to an end, its architectural interest remains, as in the case of Athens and Rome. Certainly all three buildings by Lutyens and Baker are examples of noble monuments. They deserve attention for their intrinsic architectural merit. They are also the only modern buildings in Delhi that can give us some consciousness of good architecture. Without them the capital of free India ran the risk of becoming a mere encampment of hutments and barracks.

Further, any future builder should start from these monumental examples of British buildings in India. Politically, too, we have reason to be grateful to Lutyens and Baker. For, without their work the Republic of India would have been housed in very mean quarters. As it is, it is ironical to think that, but for our own criticism in British times, these buildings would have been much finer examples of modern architecture in the new city of Delhi.

For all these reasons I plead for a revival of interest in the architecture of New Delhi. In order to support my appeal, let me give a brief account of how the core area of the new city of Delhi came up. Here, the two blocks of the Secretariat, along with Rashtrapati Bhavan (former Viceroy's House), form an inseparable unity as an acropolis or the 'high city'. This notion of an acropolis governed the design of this group of buildings from the very beginning. For political and architectural reasons it was thought to be desirable that important government buildings should command a view of the surrounding country and dominate it. The first site, chosen by the New Delhi Planning Commission, lay in a hollow ground between the village of Malcha and Talkatora Gardens. This particular area was summarily rejected by Lord Hardinge; he mentioned that he would rather not build a new capital at all than build it on that particular site.

Sir Herbert Baker, when he arrived from South Africa to collaborate with Lutyens, showed himself to be even more enthusiastic about a site dominating the surroundings. He was convinced from his study of the cities

The location for the Secretariat was chosen after much thought.

of Greco-Roman antiquity, as well as from his visit to the ancient Indian citadels, that the centre of government in New Delhi should be something like an acropolis. He quoted the biblical saying that a city set on a hill can in no way be hid. Baker had in his mind the picture of Kopje, which the union buildings set on the ridge of Pretoria presented to the eye.

The site on which all three grand buildings of New Delhi stand had been chosen by Lord Hardinge himself. To begin with, these were to be built on the Ridge. At that point in time the Viceroy wrote to Sir George Swinton, Chairman of the New Delhi Planning Commission:

> "To me personally the site on the top of the Ridge with a magnificent view over Delhi and over the whole plain, both east and west, presents very great attractions. Further, I can picture to myself the approach to Government House from the plain below with terraces, gardens and fountains along the hillside, and that should be a reproduction in miniature of Versailles and its gardens."

Parliament House, the centre of government in New Delhi.

In another letter written to Lutyens, Hardinge said: "Can you not imagine how splendid a white Government House with red tiles and gilt dome would look in such a commanding situation?"

But Lutyens had his doubts about the Ridge site. King George V, too, did not like it. The main objection was that the Ridge was too barren for trees and gardens. At first Hardinge relied on the advice of P.H. Clutterbuck (later Sir Peter), Conservator of Forests and also father of a former British High Commissioner in India. Clutterbuck thought that the Ridge could be planted with no less than seventy-two species of trees. In the end, Lord Hardinge felt that it would be a mistake to enter upon a constant struggle with nature. Finally, the new site was hit upon almost by accident in the autumn of 1912.

Lord Hardinge writes in the reminiscences of his viceroyalty:

> "I then [after rejecting the Malcha site] mounted and asked Hailey [later Lord Hailey, and then Commissioner of Delhi] to accompany me to choose a new site and we galloped over the plain to a hill some distance away. From the top of the hill there was a magnificent view embracing old Delhi and all the principal monuments situated outside the town with the River Yamuna winding its way like a silver streak at some distance. I said at once to Hailey: 'This is the site for Government House, and he readily agreed'."

This was the present site on Raisina Hill. However, Lord Hardinge noticed one difficulty. The area on top of this hill was hardly sufficient for a Government House of impressive size. One of the engineers, present at that spot, pointed out that the top could be cut off and levelled. So, this particular site on a high ground came to be finally chosen for three of the most important buildings of New Delhi. Lutyens and Baker had already seen this location and liked it after a survey of all possible locations from the back of an elephant, reminiscent of a tiger hunt.

In the first sketch that Lutyens made of the government building, the Secretariat was shown divided into two blocks but attached to Government

House. But, after the stage at which the Ridge site was proposed, the Viceroy's House became separated from the two Secretariat wings. This separation continued even when the Raisina Hill was chosen as the main site. At first only Government House was placed on the hill. However, the Secretariat was restored to its old position at the insistence of Sir Herbert Baker, who wanted to occupy the hill with the main Government House. He argued that the combination of the Secretariat with the Viceroy's House in one architectural scheme would be in harmony with the trends of British policy in India, which was moving towards reducing the autocracy of the Viceroy and giving greater importance to a government that was becoming more democratic. Thus, he emphasised, the placing of the Secretariat on the same hill along with Government House would give proper dignity and importance to the machinery of a liberal government in India.

Overlooking the Central Vista.

Rashtrapati Bhavan, floodlit.

This concept was finally adopted and two blocks of the Secretariat and the Viceroy's House became integrated into one architectural scheme, ranged around two great squares called Government Court and Viceroy's Court. They were separated by a grill. I end this chapter with a profound remark made by Sir Edwin Landseer Lutyens about the New Delhi he was to build:

"Endow your thought with faith
Your deeds with courage
Your life with sacrifice
So all men may know
The Greatness of India."

Style Matters

A new capital is always an opportunity for architecture, as can be seen at Fatehpur Sikri or Versailles. But this opportunity comes rarely. There was a stir among the architecturally-minded when the transfer to Delhi was announced and old precedents were recalled. Baker compared the move with that of Constantine the Great to Byzantium. In undertaking the work, Lutyens wondered if it would be disturbed by changes in the office of the Viceroy in the same manner as the building of St. Peter's in Rome was changed by a succession of Popes.

Two questions arose at the very beginning. First, who was to build the new city—the Public Works Department (PWD), a private firm in India, or a distinguished architect from abroad? The decision was in favour of an architect from overseas. Edwin Landseer Lutyens was a well-known name in England for designing country houses and gardens. He also happened to be married to the daughter of an ex-Viceroy of India, Lord Lytton, and King George V, too, was familiar with his name. Later, it was Lutyens who suggested the name of his friend, Herbert Baker, as a collaborator and that proposal was approved.

The second question concerned style. It was discussed and fought out with great persistence, spirit and some display of bad temper. All three buildings of the acropolis group still bear the mark of this clash of opinions and views. In a particular sense the question had almost been closed by the appointment of the architects. Both were exponents of the European Renaissance style. Baker thought that essentially New Delhi should be in this style and in an article published in *The Times*, London, wrote that all government buildings in the new city should be built according to the

Lord Hardinge expressed that the Secretariat and all other public offices should have Indian motifs.

tradition of the great Mediterranean lands, which grew out of the needs of a southern climate. Lutyens believed, above everything else, in order and was a worshipper of Newton and Wren. He thought that there was a connection between the mathematical laws of the one and the laws of architectural proportion of the other.

Lutyens was also capable of making disparaging remarks about those styles or principles that he did not like. His remarks on Indian architecture would outrage most of us: "Personally," he declared, "I do not believe there is any real Indian architecture or any great tradition. There are just spurts of various dynasties with as much intellect as there is in any other art nouveau." But that does not prevent us from enjoying his comments on Simla [now Shimla]. Contrasting the grandeur of the Himalayan settings with the buildings and planning of the summer capital of India, Lutyens remarked: "The building and conception of the place by the Public Works Department is beyond the beyond. If one was told that monkeys had built it, one could only say what wonderful monkeys—they must be shot in case they do it again."

Although both the architects were in favour of a classical European style, they had to reckon with others. An influential body of opinion wanted New Delhi to be Indo-Islamic. King George V thought that the Mughal was the style for Delhi, if not dreadfully expensive. A group of British enthusiasts of Indian art represented to the Secretary of State that the indigenous styles and crafts should have a preference over others. Even a claim of the new method of steel construction was asserted. Lord Hardinge, however, insisted on an eastern feeling in the buildings, though not on a purely Indian style. This he considered to be important from both artistic and political considerations. He wrote to Lutyens that it would be a great political blunder and also absurd to place a purely western town amid overwhelming eastern surroundings. Referring to the preference in England for the European classic style, he added: "It is not public opinion in England that is concerned, but public opinion in India." So he stressed the view that the Secretariat and all other public offices must have an Indian motif. He wanted the buildings of New Delhi to have a bold and plain character with an oriental adaptation. "You may call it bastard, or what you like," he explained, "but the only alternatives are pure Indian pure western and both are of these I would depreciate."

Besides laying down this general principle, Lord Hardinge also recommended as a model some Indian buildings he had seen such as the Hindola Mahal at Mandu. Thus Lutyens found it necessary to study the pre-existing Mughal and Hindu monuments in order to decide if they could furnish a starting point for New Delhi.

In Delhi it was generally agreed that the past should certainly not be ignored. As for Lutyens, he had serious reservations about the mixing of two styles. But, on the other hand, Baker did not have much difficulty in following this line. He told Lutyens that in a political capital the national standpoint must be recognised. Baker's advice was: "The Indian sentiment should be given preference where it does not conflict with grand principles, as the government should do." Though Baker might have appeared to be opportunistic, his own views on the architecture of New Delhi were broadly similar to that of Lord Hardinge. In his article, too, Baker had stressed that in Delhi it was neither a case for imitating Indian styles nor for following the classical orthodoxy of European architecture. Baker on the whole followed the general style of European Renaissance architecture. But, along with that style, many of the structural features of Indian architecture were grafted on, including many motifs and also decorations, which he thought expressed the myths, symbols and history of its people. That is what Baker did in the Secretariat. So when Lutyens wanted to resist the pointed arch fancied by Lord Hardinge, he wrote: "I should like to ask him [Hardinge], to what country the rainbow belongs!"

"One cannot tinker with the round arch," was a typical succinct remark of Lutyens. He continued his harangue against the pointed arch and mentioned that God did not make the eastern rainbow pointed to show his wide sympathies. Lutyens' dislike for a mix of art and politics was indeed strong. He expressed: "It is so difficult to design even a coal scuttle well; but if they bring in politics and diplomacy then it is impossible."

Baker, who recognised the claim of politics, replied: "You get your way best by showing that there are more vital things than the mere accidental shape of an arch. Un-geometrical arches and vaults do not express a scientific and logical government, which the Government of India is or should be. That is the line of attack that I think should be the most appropriate."

Lutyens was not totally opposed to the fundamental principle of synthesis. Only his idea of this synthesis was different. He did not think that a building could be made Indian by merely inserting Indian details. He particularly disliked the Viceroy's habit of taking his sketches and inserting windows of a particular type. He went on to mention that Lord Hardinge did not realise what great architecture was meant to express and also stand for. To express modern India in stone, according to Lutyens, was no easy task. Further, to represent in a building the country's amazing sense of supernatural, along with the complement of fatalism and enduring patience, almost bordered on the impossible. His conclusion was to build according to the broad principle of western architecture, but apply these principles differently in the utterly different conditions of Indian climate and bright sunshine. "If Wren had built in India," Lutyens went on to say, "it would have been something so different to anything we know of his."

Even with his rigid outlook about the style of his architecture, Lutyens was ready to integrate some of the motifs of Indian architecture such as the Buddhist stupa and its railings from Sanchi in Madhya Pradesh. He also took over the features that the Mughuls had employed to counter the fierce sunlight of India. Lutyens found that the effect of strong sunlight on all buildings in India was to destroy the colour as well as dilute the solidity of the form.

To counteract this, the Mughals had used red sandstone to protect the colour and projecting cornices, which cast broad shadows to prevent the blurring effect of the strong sunlight. Whether the Mughals had employed these devices consciously or not, Lutyens had hit upon two real optical effects successfully. These can be observed in important buildings designed by him and his team.

In the end, both Lutyens and Baker worked according to the principles adopted by each and this should be kept in mind in judging the group as a whole. Striking notes altogether different, the two Secretariat blocks were built according to one conception of synthesis. Rashtrapati Bhavan had another altogether different concept. For instance, the Rashtrapati

Rashtrapati Bhavan dome.

The ornate grill that separates Rashtrapati Bhavan from the Secretariat complex.

Bhavan dome has a simple monumental character derived from early Indian architecture. On the contrary, Baker's domes on the two Secretariat buildings are in the sophisticated Renaissance manner and somewhat complicated by more than one Indian motif. It is difficult to visualise the ensemble of three domes and two towers as the supreme harmonious unit on Raisina Hill.

Barring this criticism, which concerns the overall composition of the three important buildings of Lutyens' New Delhi, each building, when seen individually, and also from a proper perspective, does appear as an impressive example of British architecture developed in New Delhi. Baker was often criticised for the mixing of Indian and Renaissance features, but the fact remains that *chhatri*s around the main dome of Humayun's Tomb are predominately Hindu in style, while the white dome is almost a replica of the dome of Goharshad's mosque in Mashhad, Persia.

The main question is whether the combination is artistically justified or not. Both Lutyens and Baker were sincere in their efforts to find a happy synthesis between the classic European and divergent Indian styles. They have indeed added to an ensemble of impressive architecture in this historic city.

Where the President Resides

The transformation of the seat of the British Viceroy of India into the residence and office of the President of the Indian Republic is a great romance of history. It is also one of its greatest dramas. The practice of throwing the gardens open to the public for a few weeks in winter actually dates back to the British times. The Viceroy's House has now become Rashtrapati Bhavan. For a few years before this change, the Durbar Hall,

Leading to Rashtrapati Bhavan.

along with some adjacent rooms, were opened to the public as the National Museum. It exhibited some of the finest examples of ancient Indian art, including the Standing Buddha from Sarnath and the little bronze Dancing Girl from the town of Mohenjo-Daro, now in Pakistan.

It is possible to take two views of this lack of interest for a monumental building of great national interest. One may be a mistaken notion about the prestige and security of the Head of the State's residence. The other view, equally valid, would be to make the President's house play a large place in the people's imagination and the idea of a democratic India. History reveals that political greatness can hardly be found where there is not architectural greatness as well.

If this view is taken as an important point for consideration, then the insulation of Rashtrapati Bhavan is even more unfortunate. For, its builder meant the grand palace to be seen and also admired above all as an expression of a new architectural tradition for India. To many Englishmen, New Delhi was to be the symbol of Britain's imperial greatness. But Lutyens was not concerned about political motives and innuendos. He was an artist and for him the main purpose of life was to embody the idea of a divine order in the finite expression of his architecture. So he strived for creating something in New Delhi that would stand the ravages of time.

From the very beginning the work of Lutyens and Baker had to contend against two prejudices. One was found in those who looked upon New Delhi's buildings as an expression of British imperial design. The other was the affected expression of those people who thought that they could not love Indian architecture without sneering at the western. To these have been added an absence of interest and lack of discussion by the people and also the government.

Lutyens was perfectly conscious of the greatness of his task, and he wrote to his wife: "If they let me have a free hand I can please both myself and also them to get at something that may prove logical enough to stand for centuries to come." On another occasion, after referring to the great tradition of western architecture from the Greeks down to Wren, he declared: "I should have liked to have handed on that torch and made it sane for India and Indian in its character." He added: "In giving India some new sense of architectural construction, adapted to her crafts, lies the great chance of creating what may become a new and inspiring period in the history of her art."

Lutyens wanted to create this new Indian tradition by adhering to the principles of western architecture by applying them differently to suit the conditions of Indian climate and light. He did not think that by doing so he would be building something alien to India. He was quite confident that by applying Indian methods and treating western motifs for the Indian sunshine he could make them look natural in India, already rich with many architectural traditions. He also held that opinions in India would not notice or be critical of foreign elements in his architecture. He wrote: "You could employ every Indian artist, wood and stone carver in the country, to decorate and of course the fabric itself would be built by Indians. So it would only be Indian, and India must be open to new methods as some of the other countries in this world."

The validity of these arguments can hardly be challenged. Although different people might give different answers to the question whether Lutyens has succeeded in realising the high ideal he had set for himself, no one can judge his work in Delhi without making allowances for the two major disadvantages he had to face. It is easy to see that Lutyens' building fails to dominate the acropolis group as it was intended to do. Whether one takes a near view of the group from the government court, between the two blocks of the Secretariat, or further down the Central Vista, in each case Baker's Secretariat looms larger than Rashtrapati Bhavan. The eastern façade of this building is only fifty-seven feet in height and does look stunted in relation to the width of six hundred and thirty feet. Probably, about thirty feet or more added to the height of the main façade of Rashtrapati Bhavan would have made the building look more massive, as foreseen by the architect.

Rashtrapati Bhavan can hardly be seen from the Great Place (now Vijay Chowk) and it was from this very point at the end of Raisina Hill that Lutyens' building should have looked the most impressive. What one does

Rashtrapati Bhavan façade from the forecourt.

see is a broad slope of the asphalted road going up and only a blob formed by the dome of Rashtrapati Bhavan at the top. Even after ascending this slope, one cannot have a striking view of the Head of the State's palace. It is located too far away and an ornate grill, though effective, looms larger than the building it protects. On the other hand, from all points of the government square, both the South and North blocks of the Secretariat do look impressive.

But it was not Lutyens who was really responsible for these disadvantages. First of all, it was Baker who was responsible for the steep gradient, which obliterates the clear view of Rashtrapati Bhavan. He began to have misgivings about the visibility regarding the Viceroy's House soon after it was decided to place the two Secretariat buildings on Raisina Hill. But, to get over the difficulty, he proposed to take the

processional way in a gentle slope right up to the gate of the Viceroy's House. Baker got Lutyens to sign for a gradient of one in 221/2.

As soon as Lutyens realised the effect of this gradient on the Viceroy's House, he tried to persuade his friend to revise the slope. Baker had found what an advantage it would be to have a level square between his two Secretariat blocks and just would not agree to follow Lutyens' suggestions. Then the matter went to Lord Hardinge, who supported Baker rather than Lutyens. The Viceroy felt that once the house had been removed from the crest of the hill, it did not matter whether it could be seen or not. Lutyens approached King George V, who supported him. But, by that time, the Viceroy was Lord Chelmsford. Neither he nor the Government of India was inclined to take cognisance of the Emperor's privately expressed views. Lutyens never forgave Baker for this rigid attitude; Baker mentioned that this episode and the ending of a trusted friendship was the unhappiest moment of his life.

The other reason why the Viceroy's House failed to dominate the scene on the acropolis of Delhi was owing to a cut in expenditure. Lutyens was forced to revise his plans again and again. He complained bitterly that, "They cut essentials in Government House, and yet don't grudge monies to the Secretariats." Actually, Baker's buildings were also reduced, but to an extent less than that of Lutyens. So the proper ratio between the two sets of buildings got disturbed to the disadvantage of Rashtrapati Bhavan. Some years later, Lutyens appealed to Lord Reading, the new Viceroy. But Reading, too, failed to appreciate the

Secretariat slope, with Rashtrapati Bhavan in the backdrop.

Mughal Garden, Rashtrapati Bhavan.

feelings of the architect of New Delhi and refused to order any change in the approach to the Viceroy's House.

Thus, the most important building on Raisina Hill was deprived of sweeping vistas and has to be seen at close quarters to appreciate the grand scale of Lutyens' architectural design. On seeing the building after completion, someone observed, "Poor old Christopher Wren could have never done this." Whether one agrees with this sweeping remark or not, it cannot be denied that Rashtrapati Bhavan with its simple monumentality does appear to be an example of a noble architectural design.

However, the Mughal Garden of Rashtrapati Bhavan, designed by Lutyens once again, happens to be an admirable example of landscape architecture in India. At the planning stage, Lady Hardinge, the wife of the Viceroy, asked Lutyens to see the Shalimar Gardens in Lahore and Srinagar. The strong influence of the Persian gardens in Lutyens' design, according to the Char Bagh principle with waterways and fountains, can be seen clearly during the late winter months when the Mughal Garden is in full bloom and thrown open to all.

Unusual Angle

On an early summer morning of 1947, I had the unique experience of taking a slow ride right through New Delhi. It was a ride from our house, near Mori Gate of the Old City, to a bungalow next to Safdarjung's Tomb, which was almost the end of Lutyens' New Delhi at that time. My father, in his characteristic manner, had not only bought some period furniture from his English chief, but had also given me the task of fetching an old dining table loaded on a bullock cart. Though that long journey on a hot summer morning was both tedious and tough, yet the chance of seeing New Delhi, at the very end of the British rule, on an animal-driven transport was well worth the trouble.

Connaught Place, 'A' Block, 1953 and, fifty years later, in 2003.

Dominion Column and North Block, Secretariat.

After crossing congested localities such as Naya Bazaar and Ajmeri Gate of the old city, my bullock cart rattled down the slope under a typical railway bridge once known as Minto Bridge. After reaching Connaught Place the transformation of time, space and architecture was startling, when compared to the city of Shahjahanabad. Hundreds of gleaming white columns of Connaught Place going round in a circle, with the green foliage of Central Park, created a sense of elegance and order, now sadly missed while strolling around the main shopping centre of Lutyens' New Delhi.

Connaught Place and also the Circus was designed by R.T. Russel, an associate of Lutyens and opened by the Duke of Connaught. It was built on a village called Madhopur, which was once a *jagir* of the former state of Jaipur. The entire arcade at that time was replete with many elegant shops, a few departmental stores and four cinemas, all with British names, if not owners. The four cinema houses—Odeon, Plaza, Regal and Rivoli—showed only British or Hollywood films and also served as important landmarks for bus stops around that area.

As for the shops, Phelps and Ranken were among the leading European tailors of New Delhi. The Army & Navy Stores at Regal Building sold everything from expensive ladies' dresses and vintage wines, to toys such as Meccano sets and Hornby model trains. The two important pastry shops and restaurants were called Davicos and Wengers and had European owners. There was an imposing coffee house called The India Coffee House on Queensway (now Janpath). Till the end of the Second World War in 1945, this coffee house, though open to all, had mainly American soldiers occupying its tables, gulping coffee and munching doughnuts. Later, this coffee house got shifted to the lawn of a barrack called the Theatre Communication Building, which had nothing to do with theatre and was located where the present day Palika Bazaar is.

After passing the ensemble of old astronomical instruments at Jantar Mantar and the brick clock tower of the New Delhi Municipal Committee, my bullock cart trundled along Parliament Street, then an example of perfect peace and quiet. With practically no traffic except a few cars such as the Austin, Morris, Ford, or a rare Rolls-Royce, one could freely

Travelling through Connaught Place in a vintage car.

amble along that street. The only building that could be called modern on Parliament Street at that time was the Broadcasting House of All India Radio (AIR). Since my father was working there as a Talks Officer right from the British times, my brothers and I had a long association with that particular building and its studios. Apart from the Free Church, all buildings on both sides of that tree-lined street were mostly bungalows.

As the imposing Parliament House loomed ahead at the end of a carefully planned vista, the bullock cart driver decided to take a sharp turn left, near the present day Reserve Bank of India building, into a lane leading to the Old Mill Road. This detour was considered essential in view of the 'No Bullock Carts' signs all around Parliament House. (It may be of interest to my readers to know that Parliament House was designed by Herbert Baker and was originally called the Council House. The foundation stone for this unique, circular building was laid by the Duke of Connaught in 1921.

Some prominent shops of Connaught Place, 1962.

This building, with stone columns all around, is 171 metres in diameter; it is now called Sansad Bhavan.) In addition, there were mounted policemen on horseback and they could often be seen patrolling this exclusive area of Lutyens' New Delhi.

As my bullock cart managed to cross Kingsway (now Rajpath) without trouble, the vision of three edifices of British New Delhi did indeed form a beautiful sight on Raisina Hill. Some years later I came to know that the area once belonged to the Maharajah of Jodhpur and was acquired for nothing.

Lutyens and his team of architects had made two other important contributions while designing New Delhi. The significance of both these ideas could be felt as I began my return journey from the bungalow of Charles Barns, near Safdarjung's Tomb. This bungalow, typical of those designed by Lutyens' team, was indeed comfortable without any sign of even a cooler on that hot summer morning. Many trees, such as arjuna on Janpath and jamun along Ashoka Road, helped to keep me cool while I crouched under the dining table.

Parliament House, now known as Sansad Bhavan, 1955.

All India War Memorial Arch (now India Gate), Rajpath East.

Rashtrapati Bhavan, Rajpath West.

Hyderabad House, designed by Lutyens.

Soon, the All India War Memorial Arch (now India Gate), along with the marble statue of King George V, came into view just after reaching Hyderabad House. Both the War Memorial Arch as well as Hyderabad House were designed by Lutyens, along with Baroda House, a short distance away. As my bullock cart entered Hardinge Avenue, the statue of King George V under a canopy, once again designed by Lutyens, seemed to be gazing rather wistfully at the Viceroy's House, where Lord Mountbatten, the last Viceroy, was busy orchestrating the end of British rule in India.

View from Above

It was one fine morning, sometime in the mid-fifties, that I took off from Safdarjung Airport to fly around New Delhi, accompanying a group of school children going up for a joy ride. It was a rare opportunity to see an aerial view of Delhi and, in particular, New Delhi designed by Lutyens. Our aircraft was a Douglas DC-3, popularly called a Dakota, used for carrying passengers in India those days. Next to the runway was the railway line,

An aerial view of Rashtrapati Bhavan and its surroundings, circa 1935–36.

The palatial Teen Murti House, earlier known as Flagstaff House.

running alongside the airport. This was really the southern extremity of Lutyens' New Delhi.

After the take-off and a sharp turn over Chanakyapuri, till then almost barren, our pilot flew the plane along the railway lines over Lodi Colony and towards Humayun's Tomb. Then, as the plane turned north, we had a good view of the River Yamuna, Purana Qila and the Indraprastha. As I was sitting on the left, or the starboard side of the aeroplane, the entire Central Vista could be seen stretching from King George's statue and War Memorial Arch to the so-called acropolis of New Delhi on Raisina Hill. There the two blocks of the Secretariat buildings along with Rashtrapati Bhavan dominated the skyline.

Rashtrapati Bhavan certainly looked more imposing than whatever view we had got on the ground. I really wished that Edwin Lutyens could have seen the result of his impressive design high up from the air. Curiously enough, the disputed slope between the Secretariat blocks could hardly be noticed from that height and the entire city of New Delhi, as visualised by its chief architect and designer, looked well laid-out and beautiful. The roads and avenues were lined with many varieties of trees that had been chosen with care by Lutyens and his team.

Lutyens' love for mathematical order in architecture and civic design was obvious even when viewed from a swiftly moving aeroplane. The overall layout of New Delhi had a hexagonal system made up of triangles and many of the important public buildings such as Parliament House were located at the intersections of these triangles. Also, every important building of New Delhi, or even an old landmark such as Safdarjung's Tomb, had one or more roads aligned in this triangular design to provide an interesting vista at the end of a tree-lined avenue.

The only exception was the Central Vista along Kingsway. This area was laid out as a large rectangle with the War Memorial Arch at the eastern end and the Secretariat with the Viceroy's House on the western side. The view of this processional way was rendered more beautiful with long ornamental ponds and fountains at both ends. Even the tall canopy, along with King George's statue (still in position those days), appeared to be very much an integral part of the Central Vista. Our pilot, a tall Sikh gentleman with an impressive bearing, circled the plane over Jama Masjid first and then within minutes flew over the gleaming colonnade of Connaught

Statues outside the Teen Murti House.

Place with the flaming gulmohar trees in the Central Park. This park was a recreation ground during the British times and on winter weekends a military band would be in attendance here. It is sad that those flowering trees with hordes of parrots roosting on them are gone now.

After Connaught Place we flew towards Willingdon Crescent, over the Ridge and saw some buildings of various religious sentiments. Among them, prominent were the Lakshmi Narayan Temple or the Birla Mandir and two Sikh Gurdwaras—Bangla Sahib and Rakabgunj. The Catholic Church of Sacred Heart and the Church of Redemption, designed by Henry A. Medd, were located rather close to the President's House. Only the green-domed Jama Masjid of New Delhi lay hidden behind a clump of trees.

After a wonderful view of the Mughal Garden and the Circular Garden, with its round pool from which it gets its name, we saw Teen Murti House at the end of a long vista from the South Block of the Central Secretariat. That palatial building, designed by R.T. Russel, was at first the residence of the British Commander-in-Chief and was called Flagstaff House. Pandit Jawaharlal Nehru stayed there till 1964. It later became the Nehru Memorial Museum, containing in its premises an extensive library and an important centre for research.

The rich green of the garden city of Lutyens' New Delhi came to an almost abrupt end after the white marbled dome of Safdarjung's Tomb. Since our aeroplane was scheduled to land at Palam airport, instead of Safdarjung, it circled around the Qutb Minar and flew low over Mehrauli. The landscape there was extremely rugged and dotted with many tombs that were in ruins. That sight, so near New Delhi, reminded me of what Herbert Baker once said and which I had heard from the famous author and exponent on Delhi, Khushwant Singh. He recollected that Baker was aghast with the view of the selected site for New Delhi from Raisina Hill and, just as he was on the point of giving up the idea of creating impressive buildings for the new capital, a rainbow appeared on the horizon above Purana Qila. Baker took it as an omen to create two of the most impressive buildings of New Delhi.

Recording History

As chance would have it, after viewing New Delhi from the air, I came to hear about the unpromising and barren landscape around Raisina Hill from Walter Sykes George, CBE, a trusted lieutenant of Lutyens and an architect who had made New Delhi his home till the end of 1961 or early 1962. George came to Delhi when the construction of the new capital was going on in full force. He stayed on in New Delhi as a practising architect and town planner, even after India became independent in 1947. He was

Sir Walter Sykes George, centre, seen here with a group of architects and town planners, 1958.

a typical English gentleman who used to drive around Delhi in a deep green Rolls-Royce of the late twenties vintage. My brothers and I, out on our evening stroll, often saw him driving back from his office at Scindia House to his house on Alipore Road in Civil Lines. He was always dressed in a well-worn sports jacket and often had a peaked tweed cap on his head; a pair of rimless glasses was precariously balanced on the bridge of his sharp nose. The overall appearance of this elderly Englishman had a strong resemblance to Lord Elmsworth of the *Blanding Castle* stories written by P.G. Wodehouse.

In the early fifties I was familiar with George's St. Thomas' Church, near Birla Temple and came to know about his help to Lutyens and Mustoe in designing the Mughal Garden as well as planting various trees in New Delhi. But, somehow, I could not meet George till Professor T.J. Manickam, Founder Director, School of Planning and Architecture, sent me to his office. This was in February 1958 and I had to get some details about the planting

A view across the Yamuna, from Humayun's Tomb, 1958.

New Delhi, once a rocky and bare landscape!

of trees in New Delhi. It was a golden opportunity to meet someone who had worked directly with Lutyens and Mustoe.

A seminar on landscape architecture was organised by the School and one of the main speakers was George. Apart from photographing and putting up an exhibition of the important trees and some of the avenues of New Delhi, I had the privilege of recording George's impromptu speech with an early model of a tape recorder. I did the transcription in long hand and here is an excerpt of what George said at that seminar, retrieved after half-a-century from the School's journal *Urban and Rural Planning Thought* (I am grateful to the School of Planning and Architecture for allowing me to quote from this material).

George began by saying that when the announcement was made to shift the capital of India to Delhi in 1911, the profession of town planning was really in its infancy and the Government of India had no idea what the new

Once a barren landscape with a desolate look, this area was given a green cover by the architects and planners.

capital should be like. But a town plan had to be worked out with utmost urgency and what emerged for New Delhi was more a road plan than a proper 'town' plan. According to this veteran architect, the area selected for New Delhi was as rugged and rocky as Mehrauli was till the fifties of the last century. The entire site for the new city was mostly barren with some old villages that wore a desolate look. Also, the area cut up by many ravines had a large number of abandoned tombs including mosques and was not a promising area to build the most impressive capital city in the British Empire, as desired by King George V.

Since Lutyens owed his success in designing country houses to Gertrude Jekyll, an established gardener and horticulturalist, one of the things that the chief architect wanted was a list of trees that might do well in New Delhi. Getting that list was far from easy. However, along with the earlier list provided by Clutterbuck, Griessen of the horticulture service went about the task of planting the trees. But he could provide limited help as the engineers went about cutting and levelling the site rather than paying attention to saving the existing trees, or planting the new ones for the emerging city. Lutyens badly wanted a counterpart in Miss Jekyll and after some changes and Griessen's retirement, found Mustoe, a suitable and able horticulturist, to work on the new city.

George goes on to say how the work of New Delhi was directed from the site on which the present day Chelmsford Club is located; on the other side was a stone cutting mill. The road in between was called Old Mill Road. The PWD had allotted a house along with office space for the architects opposite this mill and Lutyens and Baker spent, on an average, three to four months every winter here. A large hall served as a meeting as well as a dining room. This was where everyone—lieutenant governors, architects and engineers to even plumbers—were supposed to join for the 'tiffin', as insisted by Lutyens. Since all table linen was marked with impromptu drawings by technical hands, Lutyens asked George to paint the long tabletop with blackboard paint and provide slate pencils with every plate. This not only saved the white tablecloths, but also enabled all ideas to be expressed in the form of drawings before arriving at a definite conclusion.

Central Vista with jamun trees.

As for the trees, Lutyens wanted the biggest Indian trees for the Central Vista and the jamun tree was given preference over tamarind. All roads as well as roundabouts were planted with different varieties of trees for creating a characteristic appearance for every road, roundabout or avenue. For example, Queensway was planted with arjuna; neem trees were preferred on Prithviraj Road and Aurangzeb Road. While amaltas provided colour for Windsor Place, many chukrasia trees grew very well at Mandi House. According to George, many of those trees were about thirty years old in 1958 and, though not fully grown, were largely successful in providing a green cover for most parts of New Delhi.

At the end of his illuminating exposition on trees and working with Lutyens and Mustoe, George took all the participants of that seminar, including me, for a study tour on the landscaping of New Delhi. After visiting the Central Vista, we went to Talkatora Garden, next to New Delhi's Ridge. Once there he mentioned many interesting facts regarding the planting of trees in New Delhi. Apparently these trees were watered

Persian Wheels were used for watering the trees of New Delhi—a box camera shot, 1950.

using more than one Persian Wheel driven by bullocks. We also came to know how Mustoe roamed about the Ridge and asked young George to dislodge rocks at various locations and plant some seeds himself.

Queen of England on a visit to New Delhi, 1961.

After showing us the wind-blown eucalyptus trees just outside the President's Estate, George explained that it was a classic example of wrong planting; no one had considered the strong wind, which blew from the wasteland of Haryana and Rajasthan. Later, he took us to the old government quarters laid out like barracks on Reading Road (now Mandir Marg). Since quarters for the clerical staff had to be given top priority, that area of New Delhi was completed long before the Secretariat buildings or even the Viceroy's House. As fate would have it, two minor roads in this area were once called Lutyens and Baker Road. Now for many decades since 1958 they remain nameless and forgotten.

For the field visit to the Mughal Garden, George excused himself and disappeared after hailing a taxi instead of driving back in his Rolls-Royce. A typical English gentleman, he was too modest a person to talk about his own contribution along with Mustoe in creating the most beautiful garden in New Delhi, which till today has not been surpassed.

When I met him first in the late fifties, George had already served as the first President of the Institute of Town Planners, India, as well as the Institute of Indian Architects. This grand old Englishman from the Lutyens' era received the title CBE from Queen Elizabeth on her state visit to New Delhi in 1961. Sir Walter George was truly happy with that honour. He died a few months after the investiture ceremony with not a single complaint about the city and the country he chose to live in or his personal life, which was dotted with tragedies.

Illustrating Delhi

While there were several villages surrounding old tombs and mosques in existence around Lutyens' Delhi, the one that escaped demolishment during the construction of New Delhi is known as Kotla Mubarakpur. This village, just across the railway line running south of Lodi Colony, was once leading an independent existence and had all the characteristics of many old villages scattered in and around Delhi for centuries. After 1947, Mubarakpur came to be surrounded by a number of government or government-sponsored colonies such as Sewa Nagar, or the lavishly-built Defence Colony towards the east. Just south of Kotla Mubarakpur, the

Kotla Mubarakpur—the village did not get demolished when Lutyens' Delhi was constructed.

main Ring Road now cuts across South Extension Markets I and II. In 1957 there was hardly any indication of what these markets would become.

Towards the end of summer, in 1957, a few months after I joined the School of Town and Country Planning, Professor Manickam asked me to go down to Kotla Mubarakpur and take some photographs of the village as well as the old monuments. These were needed to illustrate an article written on the basis of a socio-economic survey carried out by T.V. Sabhapathy and Professor Balakrishna Rao, then completing their diploma course in town planning. Fifty-five years later, I am thankful to them as well as to the School to allow me access to their report on Kotla Mubarakpur in *Urban and Rural Planning Thought* as well as to my illustrations.

To reach Kotla Mubarakpur from my house in Mori Gate was far from easy those days. I took an early morning bus number seventeen going to Qutb Minar-Mehrauli and got down at the crossing of Ring Road and Mehrauli Road, known as Aurobindo Marg today. Then I walked up to where the South Extension Markets now stand and, just across a bare field on which a flock of goat was passing, stood Mubarak Shah's Tomb along with an old mosque, both half hidden by village huts. Like many of the shots of Lutyens' Delhi taken a few years ago, this shot of Kotla Mubarakpur, too, was a unique and typical record of what that historic village was like those days. Since I do not have access either to original prints or negatives, only photocopies serve as a substitute of the original photographs.

Kotla Mubarakpur was a village dominated by tombs. Among these old monuments, three are rather prominent and date back to the Lodi and Syed dynasties. The most important among them is the tomb of Sultan Mubarak Shah of the Syed dynasty who was put to death in AD 1433. This octagonal tomb, surrounded by an arched colonnade, was built in his memory by his successor. Around the main building there were ruined enclosure walls and relics of gateways with a few large neem trees growing near them. Close to this enclosure is a mosque with three typical domes of that particular period. In the western periphery of this village and a short distance away I could

Left to right: A thatched house next to Mubarak Shah's Tomb; view of Hira Singh Road, the only metalled road in Kotla Mubarakpur, 1957.

find two more tombs dating from the Lodi period. They were supposed to be of kings from the Lodi period and were known as Chhote Khan and Bada Khan.

According to the report of T.V. Sabhapathy and Professor Balakrishna Rao, (the latter was my colleague in the School of Planning and Architecture for some years), the village of Kotla Mubarakpur had developed only after the fifteenth century; in 1956-57, it had a population of only three thousand five hundred and forty or so, distributed among six hundred families. What is even more amazing by today's standard is the average earning of Rs 120 per month for ninety per cent of the population; only 2.4 per cent had monthly incomes ranging from Rs 300 to Rs 500. Till the late fifties there was no domestic electric supply, along with piped water supply or a sewage system and the villagers drew water from open wells. For those who could afford it, there were private wells fitted with hand pumps.

On that particular day of 1957, when I walked up to the centre of Mubarakpur, I saw the scene of a typical village surrounding Delhi—elders smoking hookah sitting on their *charpoys*, or stringed cots, surrounded by children. Even the stone platform all around Mubarak Shah's Tomb had several *charpoys* scattered across. These were clearly in use every day and night. The only metalled street, named Hira Singh Road, was not more than twenty feet wide and had brick-built shops of rather low standard. Ramshackle wooden and bamboo stalls jutted into both sides of that narrow road. At the end of this road, where it opened up near Sewa Nagar, I saw many brick buildings coming up. The women residents of those buildings were washing their clothes on cement platforms running along that street. Soiled water flowing in a black stream down the street made a most unpleasant view.

Fifty years later, in July 2007, I was once again given an assignment to photograph Mubarak Shah's Tomb and other old monuments around Kotla Mubarakpur. The photographs were required to illustrate a book written by Rakhshanda Jalil on the lesser known monuments of Delhi. It was titled *Invisible City: The Hidden Monuments of Delhi*. After having read the draft of her manuscript, I equipped myself with a solid pair of footwear as she had warned in her writings that her feet had got mucked up while walking about Kotla Mubarakpur in only a pair of slippers.

Today, it is unbelievable that this typical old village, so near Lutyens' Delhi, has become the biggest centre for selling timber, plywood and other building material from haphazardly constructed shops and how the monuments are neglected here and are turning into ruins. When I was searching for Mubarak Shah's Tomb among a labyrinth of lanes, there were not only cesspools everywhere but heaps of garbage piled up at the nooks and corners of practically every building. Mubarak Shah's Tomb was fenced in with iron grills and the locked gate had no signs of the guard appointed by the Archaeological Survey of India (ASI). Even with an ultra wide-angle lens on my camera, I could hardly do justice to that impressive monument and had to be satisfied with a partial shot.

Eye of the Camera

"Those days [1942-1952] Parliament Street was really a wonderful tree-lined avenue with no multi-storey buildings around. Only Parliament House appeared at the end of a carefully planned vista." That is what I observed in my book *Delhi: Light, Shades, Shadows*, published in 2005. Continuing on the same note, I wrote, "The motor traffic on that important street of New Delhi was negligible at all hours and one could walk across without any concern." Unbelievable, as it may appear now, that was the reality of that street when I walked or cycled to Broadcasting House where my father worked till 1952. From 1962 onwards I used to often drive my Lambretta scooter next to Broadcasting House, Akashvani Bhavan, to meet T. Kasinath, the then Director of Photo Division, Government of India. He had just taken over as Director and no matter how busy he was, his room was an open house for all photographers, young and old. Broadcasting House, along with the new Reserve Bank of India building, were the only modern buildings on Parliament Street then.

All India Radio moved to its new headquarters, the New Broadcasting House, in February 1943. Till then it used to operate from an old bungalow at 18 Alipore Road, Civil Lines. Unlike other important buildings in and around Raisina Hill and the Central Vista, the New Broadcasting House was constructed not with off-white granite or red sandstone, but with bricks and double pillars cast in concrete. Even the colour scheme of this unusual building was different, with the vivid red of the painted bricks contrasting with the pale cream of the plastered concrete. This change in building material was necessary because of the high cost of stone and its transportation problems during World War II.

Broadcasting House, lit up.

For such a radical building, both in its look and concept, the credit should go to the first Chief of AIR, Sir Lionel Fielden. Sir Lionel was sent to India in 1935 to organise radio broadcasting in India. He, along with his assistants Zulfiquar and his brother Ahmed Shah Bokhari, made AIR a dynamic institution. It was Ahmed Shah Bokhari, the first Indian Controller of AIR, who had persuaded my father to join the Central News Organisation of AIR. When Father became the Talks Officer there, in 1944, he often sent me to AIR with his home-written script when not inclined to go to his office or, after 1947, when he was busy writing his famous book, *The Autobiography of an Unknown Indian*.

Broadcasting House, those days, was one of those rare government buildings that required a pass to enter its impressive portals. However, that rule was not applicable to me. As a youngster who had just completed fourteen and was less than five feet in height, the guard knew that I was heading for the room of Charles Barns, the Director, or his PA,

Traffic under Hardinge Bridge, 1961-62.

Mrs. Khinsaw. Broadcasting House was also unique in another respect. It had a lift whose fittings shone like a mirror and was maintained in a spick-and-span condition, unlike the lifts in other government buildings.

Going regularly to All India Radio's office on Parliament Street and later working at All India Fine Arts & Crafts Society (AIFACS) till the late fifties of the last century gave me a lot of opportunities to observe as well as take

Passengers on an elephant and in a bus, on a New Delhi road, 1958.

part in the activities around that important street of New Delhi. As I wrote in my earlier book on Delhi, "On regular office days, two cycle tracks [they were the first to come up in Delhi] running on both sides of this road used to swarm with thousands of cyclists pedalling their way to the Secretariat in the morning." Describing the traffic, I continued: "The motor traffic on that important street of New Delhi was negligible at all hours and one could walk across without any concern…As for the cars, they were mostly little Austin or Morris, with a sprinkling of large American cars such as Ford V-8 and Oldsmobile." At times, even luxury cars such as a Bentley, or a Rolls-Royce, usually belonging to the princely states, could be seen rolling up and down Parliament Street. Bus numbers five or nine, which were supposed to ply till the Secretariat from Old Delhi, were irregular and more often than not none could be seen even after an interval of an hour or so.

Just as one crossed Regal Building, which had a number of interesting shops such as Simla Studios and eating joints such as Kwality Restaurant, one came across a circle in front of Jantar Mantar called Narendra Place. On one side was a group of flats called Wenger's flats and on the other side, at the site of Park Hotel, was another row of two-storeyed flats, where several media persons such as Gargirani Mahajan of AIR, the late Rakshat Puri, a poet and columnist and his wife Meenakshi, an art critic, had their residences. After Narendra Place, on the right-hand side, was the brick building of the New Delhi Municipal Committee, with its well-known clock tower, now demolished.

There was not a single multi-storeyed building on Parliament Street till Broadcasting House and it was only around 1955 that the massive Reserve Bank of India building was constructed with two statues of Yaksha and Yakshi by the well-known artist from Santiniketan, Ramkinkar Baij, at the main entrance. Shortly afterwards came Akashvani Bhavan, the headquarters for All India Radio, which began to broadcast television programmes, mainly educational, for schools of Delhi and New Delhi.

After a gap of almost sixty years, my association with Broadcasting House was renewed thanks to the initiative taken by fellow mass communicators,

Reserve Bank of India building, Parliament Street and the famous Yaksha and Yakshi sculptures by Ramkinkar Baij.

many of whom had been my students at the Indian Institute of Mass Communication. I had the privilege of broadcasting and reaching out to a wider audience while visiting Broadcasting House, something that I could never imagine in my early years.

Speaking a Thousand Words

All the rulers of Delhi have left their mark in the form of buildings ranging from forts, palaces and mosques to impressive monuments such as the Humayun's Tomb. In this respect Pandit Jawaharlal Nehru was no exception. After India became a sovereign republic in 1951 and the First Five-Year Plan came into operation in 1952, New Delhi witnessed a sudden growth of palatial government buildings and many cultural centres, both government and autonomous. As for me, I could see this tremendous development all over Lutyens' Delhi when I joined AIFACS sometime in 1956 as a photographic assistant.

Krishi Bhavan, one of the first high-rise buildings to come up on Rajpath.

Before that, my visits to Lutyens' Delhi were somewhat random and restricted to two things—buying exotic delicacies for my father's parties from shops such as the Empire Store in Connaught Place, which has now disappeared and seeing art and photographic exhibitions at AIFACS' improvised display hall. At that time AIFACS was located in an abandoned war-time church on Parliament Street. I saw occasional films, mostly documentaries, or classics such as *Hamlet*, directed and acted by Sir Lawrence Olivier, at Odeon, Plaza or Regal. These cinema halls were the oldest and showed English films mostly from Hollywood or England. The first two romantic films that I saw with my three fellow students from Miranda House were *Roman Holiday* and *Three Coins in the Fountain*. Both these were screened at the smallest cinema hall of New Delhi, near Regal, called Rivoli.

Soon after I passed out of Delhi University with a Bachelor of Science Honours degree, my family circumstances, along with the realisation that I would not be a success if I studied pure science, steered me not to join a Master of Science course. This decision left me with ample free time and almost every day I walked up to Connaught Place to read at the British Information Services or the United States Information Service (USIS) library. Once there, books on photography and magazines such as *Amateur Photographer* or *Popular Photography* had my preference. In addition, I usually got engrossed with some of the contemporary illustrated magazines such as *Life* or *National Geographic*. A British magazine called *Picture Post*, too, was my favourite. I learnt a lot from going through many of their photo features usually by famous photojournalists such as Robert Capa, Eugene Smith and, of course, Henri Cartier Bresson. Photographs by these masters, mostly black-and-white those days, had a profound influence on me as an upcoming photojournalist working in his spare time.

As far as I can remember, Krishi Bhavan and Udyog Bhavan were the first high-rise buildings to come up on either side of Rajpath. As chance would have it, I got an opportunity to visit Krishi Bhavan for an interview in the summer of 1956 and, a few months later, quite unexpectedly had a chance to work in AIFACS. By that time AIFACS had shifted to its new

The All India Fine Arts & Crafts Society (AIFACS) building.

building, just across the roundabout, touching Krishi Bhavan. For going to the office I would often get down from the bus in front of the Reserve Bank of India building in Parliament Street. This building had come up on the site of a demolished government bungalow with a large garden. Just across Parliament Street was Broadcasting House.

The narrow road, which branched off from Parliament Street and after taking a sharp turn to the right went up to Rajpath and finally ended near the Sunehri Bagh Mosque, was Old Mill Road first and then renamed Rafi Ahmed Kidwai Marg. When I walked down Rafi Marg, on my right was the nondescript and rather dull office of the Indian Newspaper Society. In contrast, the next building of the Council of Scientific and Industrial Research was designed by a brilliant architect, the late Achyut Kanvinde and is one of the best examples of modern architecture in Delhi. Then finally, at the end of the Old Mill Road and touching the roundabout was my destination, AIFACS. It had multiple exhibition halls and an auditorium with the latest lighting equipment. My late friend, Sitangshu Mukherjee, was in charge of not only the lighting equipment but also the auditorium and many of the theatrical and dance performances that took place in that hall.

There was tremendous development all over Lutyens' Delhi in the fifties.

The Supreme Court, 1958.

Before AIFACS, the only other auditorium that had opened in Delhi was on the top floor of the Indian Council of World Affairs (ICWA), located at Sapru House, at the end of Barakhamba Road. ICWA was inaugurated by Pandit Jawaharlal Nehru in May 1955. One of the first theatre groups to perform there was Bouhurupee from Calcutta, founded by the famous theatre personality Shambhu Mitra. The play was *Rakta Karabi*, by Rabindranath Tagore.

Within a few years, the roundabout, popularly known as Mandi House, had almost an explosion of cultural centres—Sangeet Natak Akademi for the performing arts, Sahitya Akademi for literature and Lalit Kala Akademi for the visual arts. All these were established in quick succession in 1953 and 1954. They were housed in Rabindra Bhavan when the building, designed

Shri Ram Centre for Art and Culture (top) and Rabindra Bhavan, two iconic centres of culture.

Office of the Accountant General of India, Indraprastha Estate, 1963.

by the well-known government architect Habibur Rahman, was completed. At first it seemed that Pandit Nehru was not happy with the initial design created by Habibur Rahman; he wanted to have a building housing the academies with more Indian characteristics. Finally, a compromise had to be worked out. The other cultural centres around Mandi House are Triveni Kala Sangam, Shri Ram Centre for Art and Culture and Bharatiya Kala Kendra along with the Kamani Auditorium.

Another institutional area that began to be developed rapidly was the Indraprastha Estate or ITO as it is popularly called. The name ITO is an abbreviation of the income tax office. Actually, the correct name for this group of buildings is the Indian Revenue Building. Till the seventies it was not just the main office for income tax officers but the customs house for clearing airline baggage and probably the sales tax commissioner's office as well.

Indian Industries Fair, 1961.

The campus of the Indian Institute of Public Administration was one of the first to come up at the Indraprastha Estate on the Ring Road just before Firoz Shah Kotla. Then came the office of the Accountant General of India and that truly impressive building was also designed by Habibur Rahman. The town planning building of the School of Planning and Architecture was constructed later. Professor Humayun Kabir, then the Education Minister, laid the foundation stone for this building in the summer of 1958 and the School shifted from its Mansingh Road hutments and Delhi Polytechnic to its new premises. Within two years, the Ministry of Education of the Government of India decided to merge the department of architecture of Delhi Polytechnic in Kashmiri Gate with the town planning school. The new name of this premier institution of New Delhi became the School of Planning and Architecture or SPA for short. Thanks to the influence of our director Professor Manickam on the government, a prime spot was allotted to this building.

Professor Manickam, with his dynamic vision, made photography a compulsory subject for all under- and post-graduate students. This merger had a beneficial influence in my career. After being chosen as a junior member of the faculty, I began to take classes with great enthusiasm. Many of the outstanding professors of architecture and town planning in India and abroad still recognise my contribution to their knowledge and till this date call me Guruji, which I cherish even after a gap of more than half-a-century.

The profound influence of Pandit Nehru on Delhi's town planning and architecture was obvious when he opened a conference on town planning in Bangalore (now Bengaluru). I had not only the opportunity to photograph the Prime Minister of India from close quarters, but also project colour slides for a presentation on the Delhi Master Plan that I had prepared under the guidance of the eminent town planner Syed S. Shafi.

The other two buildings of New Delhi where I would often see Pandit Nehru were Vigyan Bhavan, completed in 1956 for the plenary session of UNESCO and also the acoustically perfect auditorium of the National

Purana Qila, at the east end of Lutyens' Delhi.

Physical Laboratory, near the Pusa Institute for Agriculture. Off and on, and particularly during the winter months, maestros such as Yehudi Menuhin, Louis Kentner and Herbert von Karajan conducting the Vienna Philharmonic Orchestra, could be heard in those two halls, where Pandit Nehru accompanied by his daughter Indira Gandhi listened to European classical music with rapt attention and, during intervals, mingled with the audience.

New Delhi, Framed

In the autumn of 1956, after a spell of torrential rain that lasted nearly a week, Delhi was jolted by a severe earthquake at about ten at night. Though the duration of the quake was less than a minute, many of the books piled up on a shelf above the divan I was dozing on tumbled down. I ran to my parent's room to see if they were awake. The next morning, when I opened the newspaper (there was no radio in our house), apart from the main news about the earthquake, a small news item in one corner caught my

A view from Jantar Mantar, 1979.

New Delhi Railway Station, 1956.

attention. A leopard and a bear cub had arrived at the newly-opened Delhi Zoo. Before that there were only a few spotted deer and a pair of *neelgais*, or blue bulls, in an open enclosure just under the southern gate of Purana Qila, or the Old Fort.

Since I was a young graduate at large with no worries, except for a perpetual shortage of funds, I immediately set out for Sunder Nagar, next to Purana Qila, with my Perkeo camera, which had a few unexposed frames. I had recently done a feature on the Indian Railway for Khushwant Singh, then Chief Editor of a government magazine called *Yojana*. After entering the zoo through an improvised gate next to Sunder Nagar, and walking to a clump of babul trees, I saw a khaki-clad man huddled below one such tree, imploring an animal, which I thought to be a monkey, to come down. When I looked up, there was no trace of the monkey. Instead, a leopard cub was staring straight down at me belligerently. This was most surprising for a cub of that size.

Just after I took a shot of that young leopard, he leapt from the tree and, paying no heed to the keeper's shout to come to him, hid under a thick bush. For me there was no other alternative than to walk away quietly from that spot. I could hear the rustic keeper shouting behind me for disturbing the mental peace of his animal ward. A short distance away, on a patch of grass, I came across a chubby bear cub, tied to a wooden wedge driven firmly into the ground. That baby bear, busy gnawing a twig or a fruit, suddenly leapt at a beautiful lady dressed in a silk sari with a baby boy in

Indrani Rahman with her son, Ram, at the Delhi Zoo, 1956.

her arms. She was trying her best to get her little boy interested in that bear cub, but the baby's face looked as if he was far from amused. Weeks later, I recognised her as the famous dancer Indrani Rahman and the baby boy is now my famous photographer friend, Ram Rahman.

From those humble beginnings in 1956, Delhi Zoo underwent a total transformation by 1959. If my memory serves me right, the architect who designed many of the interesting structures such as the main gate as well as some of the enclosures was Habib Rahman, Ram Rahman's father. About the same time I had the good fortune of meeting the landscaping and gardening advisor to the Delhi Zoo, Mr Hatashita, in my father's house. There was another portly young man from Japan, whose name I cannot recollect, who had also worked on the same project.

One winter morning of 1959 I somehow managed to borrow a state-of-the-art 35mm camera, a Leica M-3, from Simla Studios. That studio, located in Regal Building, was one of the best; its people were also very friendly and cooperative to young photographers. On that particular day, thanks to the kindness of the late Devraj Chopra, the manager, I was able to borrow a 135mm telephoto lens. As for 35mm films, Devraj knocked off four rupees from the retail price of twenty rupees for a colour film called Kodachrome and also gave me a black-and-white roll free.

However, in spite of an expensive telephoto lens and colour film loaded into the Leica camera, what gave me a prize-winning shot was a black-and-white one

Himalayan black bear at the Delhi Zoo, 1959.

Group of elephants seen against the southern gate of Purana Qila. Photo: Malabika

taken with my humble Voightlander Vito-B, costing less than two hundred rupees. The subject of that shot was the same Himalayan black bear cub seen with Indrani and Ram Rahman nearly three years ago. He was now a full-size animal and had climbed high on a dried-up tree to watch if his breakfast of fruits had arrived.

A few years later, the Delhi Zoo campus, spread across acres of land, had become a happy hunting ground (not in the way Jim Corbett used that phrase) for my would-be wife, Malabika's twin lens reflex camera and also my Exacta Varex that had a telephoto lens. But what created a bit of a tussle between us was that while I could take close-ups of animals such as tigers or lions easily with the telephoto lens, Malabika had to be satisfied with only a 75mm fixed lens on her Rolliecord. The biggest joke among us was that, in spite of the limitation of her camera, Malabika soon managed to take three striking pictures of Delhi Zoo and those photographs were soon accepted for publication in newspapers such as *The Statesman*. Even today, the picture of a group of elephants seen against the southern gate of Purana Qila is exhibited and admired.

After our daughter Satarupa was born, Delhi Zoo was our favourite picnic spot, especially during the winter months. But like many other attractive parks and gardens of New Delhi, the unruly crowd of visitors frequenting the Zoo became distressing. Maneka Gandhi's edicts when she was the Environment Minister did nothing to improve the lot of either the animals or the garden of Delhi Zoo and we seldom went there, except to watch migratory birds.

Chanakyapuri, or Diplomatic Enclave, was the westernmost area coming up near Lutyens' Delhi. It was also the latest as well as the most exclusive. By the late fifties of the last century, the British High Commission, the American and Russian Embassies as well as many other chanceries of European and Asian countries had their embassy buildings in the posh Chanakyapuri area of New Delhi. Since it was an almost impossible task to photograph them all I chose to work mainly on the three buildings that I found to be the most photogenic. These were the American, the Swiss and the Swedish Embassies. Though I could take a very good aerial shot of the British High Commission, from the top of Ashok Hotel, I found that building to be rather dull and prosaic and shudder to think how Lutyens would have reacted to it.

Once, while illustrating an article on New Delhi, written by the well-known journalist and film critic Amita Malik, I took a photograph of the American chancery in daylight. After seeing a black-and-white bromide print, which was technically perfect, she remarked, "Dhruva, where has the magic of your architectural photography gone?" And that made me realise that the exceptional charm of the architect Edward D. Stone's creation required different lighting arrangements other than just sunlight. Around that time President Dwight D. Eisenhower, the first American president to visit India, drove up to Rashtrapati Bhavan from Vijay Chowk in a sky-blue Packard car with Pandit Jawaharlal Nehru. As the car passed, I fired a single flash bulb fixed on my camera flash gun. The picture was technically perfect and was reproduced in a few newspapers in Delhi. In those days expandable flash bulbs were expensive and also needed time for their replacement and there was just no chance of doing a retake while working with subjects such as the US President and the Prime Minister of India.

Soon after my attempt at news photography that evening went off well, I got a brainwave to see if the US Embassy was floodlit for that occasion. So I decided to walk down the road once called King George's Avenue up to the Teen Murti circle. After entering Chanakyapuri and the Nyaya Marg roundabout, I could see the American Embassy lit up in all its glory. To capture that exciting vision, I went right up to the front gate and set up the light tripod that was always in my camera bag. A lone guard standing at the gate casually asked if I was a press photographer and stepped aside to give me a clear view of the embassy building. Today, it is impossible to imagine that a decent shot of the American Embassy can be done with such ease and finesse.

A dramatic shot of the American Embassy, floodlit, 1959.

The Swiss Embassy.

In the next two years I was a constant visitor, usually accompanied by my newly-married wife, to photograph many of the interesting embassy buildings of this unique area of New Delhi. Among them, I particularly liked working in and out of the embassy buildings of Sweden and Switzerland. The Swedish chancery was designed by architects S. Lindstrom and Jöran Curman and landscaped by Walter Bauer. It was opened in 1959 in the presence of Pandit Nehru.

Chanakyapuri, even after half-a-century, is still one of the most beautiful and well-kept areas of New Delhi. You get to see many interesting examples of contemporary architecture here, ranging from artist Satish Gujral's Belgian Embassy to the traditional Dzong style of architecture of the Bhutan Embassy.

Caught on Camera

On a biting cold morning of 26 January 1959, the view of the Central Vista from the top of India Gate, once called the All India War Memorial Arch, was truly exciting and new. At the distant horizon, Rashtrapati Bhavan, flanked by the two identical twins, the Secretariat buildings, were gleaming through the winter mist. A crowd of thousands of men, women and children had gathered all along Rajpath, waiting for the President's coach to roll down Raisina Hill. Every single soul stood with bated breath for the tenth Republic Day parade to march down Rajpath. For me it was not only a rare opportunity to use my cameras for the first time to photograph that national event, but also to see Lutyens' New Delhi from a vantage point, which will always be considered unique.

The idea for the All India War Memorial Arch was first suggested in 1917 and the actual construction work commenced in 1921, some three years after the First World War ended. This arch came up to put on record the names of 70,000 Indian fallen soldiers of that war along with 13,516 others who had died at the North West Frontier and Middle Eastern combat. Since Lutyens had already designed the Cenotaph at Whitehall of London, he was assigned the building of this commemorative arch as well. In the overall concept, the appearance and location of the War Memorial Arch, at one end of King's Way, had a strong resemblance to the Arc de Triomphe of Paris.

Walking around the narrow causeway at the top of India Gate, I could see more than one example of Lutyens' architectural expressions. Down below at a short distance was the sandstone canopy with King George's marble statue. About a week or two earlier I had seen a number of workers

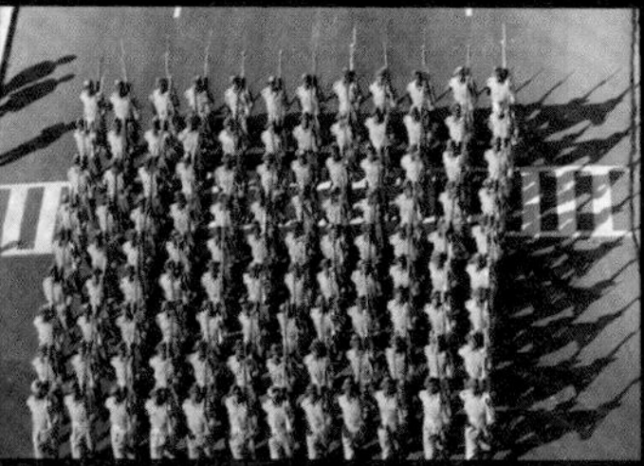

Top to bottom: Republic Day celebrations, viewed from above India Gate; Republic Day, 1959.

cleaning up the statue while crawling up on a temporary scaffolding and the entire scene resembled a busy beehive. At some distance, Hyderabad House and Baroda House could be seen as two examples of Lutyens' design. After Independence, one became a guesthouse for foreign dignitaries while the other was turned into an office of the Northern Railways.

Beyond King George's statue was the first and only sports stadium of New Delhi, built at the insistence of Lady Willingdon and also named after her. This ugly and prosaic façade of exposed brick not only ruined the appearance of the eastern end of Kingsway but also blocked the impressive view of Purana Qila. However, high up from the arch, the two gates of Purana Qila did appear imposing and formed an impressive backdrop to the grandiose processional approach at the end of Rajpath.

Hearing the distant clip-clop of the horses of the President's guards was the signal for me to move over to the western side of the arch and view Dr Rajendra Prasad, the first President of India, reaching the saluting base in an open coach, flanked by colourful guards who were largely ceremonial in those peaceful years. The booming sound of the twenty-one-gun salute for the President reminded me of the first Independence Day on 15 August 1947 when, as a fourteen-year-old boy, standing among a cheering crowd of many thousands, I had witnessed the unfurling of the national flag on the crowd-filled lawns right under India Gate. The only event that I could photograph on that historic evening was the fly-past by a group of Spitfire fighter planes. It was that obsession that made me miss the appearance of a rainbow, which had been pointed out by Lord Mountbatten to Pandit Nehru. The national flag was unfurled by a young army officer after hearing a remote-control bell rung actually by the Prime Minister and not by Governor General Mountbatten.

King George's statue, near India Gate, 1959.

A rainy day at Minto Bridge, near Connaught Place, 1956.

Returning once again to the Republic Day of 1959, I could see that the President, Dr Rajendra Prasad, was not only being received by Prime Minister Nehru, but also by the Defence Minister, V.K. Krishna Menon, who took particular care in his movements and gestures to attract the attention of the dignitaries and the general public assembled for the event.

The Republic Day parade ended that year with the first supersonic bang over New Delhi from a Gnat fighter plane, which the Indian force had just acquired. Then, I began my walk among the milling crowd towards the Janpath crossing, where stood the National Archive building, designed by Sir Edwin Lutyens himself. This particular office was once called the Imperial Archives and the massive squat building in cream and red sandstone was the only one of the four proposed at the crossing of Kingsway and Queensway; the three meant for a museum and other cultural activities remained only on paper for more than a decade after India became independent and also a republic. Further down Queensway, after a large roundabout, once called the Windsor Place, two identical buildings were known as the Eastern and Western Courts. These two buildings were the creations of the architect R.T. Russel, who is known more for his work in designing Connaught Place and the Teen Murti House, then the residence of Prime Minister Pandit Nehru and earlier, when called the Flagstaff House, was the residence of the British Commander-in-Chief.

The Western Court still functions as a government hostel with an impressive exterior, but all rooms and services have gone down really beyond even reasonable expectations. It earlier had a distinct European ambience. Even till the late fifties it had a full four-course buffet lunch including a choice of soups, followed by a cold meat platter along with salad, and finally a caramel pudding or jelly, ending with unlimited coffee taken with hot discussions on various policies of the Government.

While one can understand the Western Court's inclination for the British way of living because of its origin since the days of the imperial rule, another hostel run by the Government after the independence of India was

The Western Court, Janpath.

the Constitution House on Curzon Road, now Kasturba Gandhi Marg. In spite of its grandiose name, this hostel was originally nothing more than several rows of single rooms for army officers with a common bathroom between two individual rooms. This utilitarian and yet a peculiar layout at times led to many awkward situations when adjacent rooms came to be occupied by individuals of opposite sex and also gave rise to several juicy stories being circulated among many of the occupants.

But, on the plus side, Constitution House—along with the Constitution Club—was a unique institution of New Delhi where government officials, both men and women, along with artists, musicians and also individuals with different religious backgrounds, such as the first Baha'i representative in India, stayed in perfect harmony, eating meals that were fairly tolerable at the canteen as well as entertaining their friends. It was sad to see this shabby yet interesting landmark give way to a multiple-storeyed cluster of tiny government flats, hardly better than rows and rows of pigeonholes.

Returning once again to the Janpath of January 1959, that road made me think about the Queensway of certain winter afternoons of 1943. My father was doing some research on Islamic history and architecture and he would often visit the libraries of the Imperial Archive and also the Archaeological Survey of India. To reach there we had to walk from the Archive building down Queensway to the bus or the shared *tonga* stand in front of Odeon cinema. After the stately Western and Eastern Court buildings, Imperial Hotel, with its modern appearance, was once the only luxury European hotel of New Delhi. This hotel was declared open sometime in the 1930s. And, in spite of its name and the fact that it offered ultimate luxury in the colonial style of hospitality, it provided facilities and accommodation for Mahatma Gandhi, Pandit Nehru and Muhammad Ali Jinnah to discuss the partition of India with Lord Mountbatten. Here, Jawaharlal Nehru's family had a permanent suite at their disposal.

Queensway, later renamed Janpath, had a series of shanty shops that were set up by refugees from West Punjab after the partition of India. More often than not those shops sold trendy footwear, especially ladies' sandals and slippers, at unbelievably low prices that would attract many visitors from Mumbai and Kolkata. It was perhaps an irony of fate that more than one shop of British origin, Sutherlands or Allied Motors, was still selling Wedgwood china and Rolls-Royce cars opposite this improvised refugee market.

Reaching the last end of Janpath on that morning, I could not help but sit down at a wobbly table of India Coffee House. This ever-popular premise had shifted from Queensway to a somewhat ramshackle and even more plebian location on the lawn of Theatre Communication Building. This building got its peculiar name because it was the communication centre for eastern theatre during World War II. Among many English officers working there was Aubrey Bond, author Ruskin Bond's father.

At the place where Janpath joined Connaught Circus stood Scindia House, one of the tallest buildings in and around Connaught Place at that time. It had no less than four electric lifts, a luxury among Delhi buildings. Scindia House also had a large number of well-known shops— Ranken and Co, the best and oldest outfitters; Cooke & Kelvey, the jeweller and silverware shop, along with Oxford Book Shop. As for cars, aside from Allied Motors for Rolls-Royce and Bentley, there was Premnath Motors, dealing mostly in Fiat, the first compact car that came to India after the Second World War. After turning left from the Scindia House junction there was Regal Building; this is where Parliament Street, now renamed Sansad Marg, began.

Divine Images

Whichever dynasty or ruler came to Delhi, inevitably one of the first buildings they put up was an imposing structure for public worship such as a temple, a mosque or a church. In Lutyens' Delhi, there were two cathedral churches, an imposing modern temple along with three old ones, as well as a small mosque next to Parliament House, besides the many old ones scattered from Lodi Road to nooks and corners of Central Vista. There were also two imposing gurdwaras, within a stone's throw from Parliament House.

Cathedral Church of Redemption, designed by Henry A. Medd.

Gurdwara Bangla Sahib, near Parliament House.

When New Delhi was built, the Cathedral Church of Redemption, just west of the Parliament House and a short distance from the Jaipur Column, came up mainly because of the initiative taken by Lord Irwin. Henry A. Medd, working with Lutyens, was the architect who designed this church. He was inspired by the Palladio's Church of Il Redentore in Venice as well as Lutyens' St. Jude's Church in Hamstead Heath Garden Suburb. It was built with a combination of sandstone and brick and, instead of the pointed spire of a church, it has a small dome topping the church tower. Once inside, high arches all along the aisle and topped by a high roof create an impressive atmosphere, truly befitting a house of god. In the summer months of 1955 I had a chance to explore this cathedral and also find how cool and comfortable it remained in that season. It stands as a peaceful oasis on Church Lane. Shortly after appearing for my B.Sc. examination in 1955, I would often hitch a ride from Reverend John, then the Vicar of the Church of Redemption, who was a member of the Cambridge Brotherhood near Mori Gate. Father John had a little Ford Prefect car given to him by his parish members. While driving to his church, at times he would suggest that we stop at Madras Coffee House, opposite Statesman House in Connaught Circus. Once there, we would share a plate of *vada* or *idli* with the smallest cups of coffee and pay a bill of less than a rupee by taking out whatever coins we had in our pockets. It was amazing indeed to see what a simple and frugal life these priests led even in Delhi.

Since the Church of Redemption belonged to the Anglican or the Protestant Order, Father Luke, who was from the Catholic Franciscan order, took the initiative to organise the building of a Roman Catholic cathedral right next to Gol Dak Khana, or the General Post Office of New Delhi. Sacred Heart Cathedral, once again designed by Henry A. Medd, came up around 1930. However, the architectural style as well as the appearance of this cathedral, though designed by the same architect, happen to be totally different from its Anglican counterpart, the Church of Redemption. The interesting characteristics of this church are two tall towers on both sides of the entrance, rising high above the curved ceiling, built in the classical Italian style.

Lakshmi Narayan Temple, also known as Birla Temple.

The two-and-a-half-acre campus of the Sacred Heart Cathedral, acquired by Father Luke, has two of the best public schools of New Delhi—Convent of Jesus and Mary for girls, which is right next to the church, and St. Columba's for boys. This road, once named Baird Road, leads to a hexagonal market building called Gole Market, one of the oldest in New Delhi. On the left was Reading Road, now renamed Mandir Marg. This particular road, running all along the eastern side of the New Delhi Ridge, not only has the most important and largest temple of New Delhi, the Lakshmi Narayan Temple, or more popularly called the Birla Temple, but also New Delhi's Bengali Kali Bari, or the temple of Ma Kali, a manifestation of Durga Ma. This temple, the first Kali Bari of New Delhi, was established in 1930 and completed in 1931. The first President of Kali Bari Society was no less a person than Netaji Subhash Chandra Bose.

When we came to Delhi in 1942, after about a year or so we had hordes of visitors, mostly from Kolkata. Among all the tourist spots they wanted to visit after Qutb Minar was Birla Mandir. This popular landmark of New Delhi, dedicated to God Narayan and Goddess Lakshmi, was built by the famous business family of Birlas. While the construction of this temple in *Nagara* style had began as early as 1933, this imposing temple was finally opened by Mahatma Gandhi in 1939. Before agreeing to inaugurate the temple, he made it a condition that people of all caste and creed should be allowed to enter and worship here.

As we go down Mandir Marg towards Paharganj, there are two more places of worship of completely different faiths. Nearest to Birla Temple is the first Buddhist temple of New Delhi. This Maha Bodhi Society temple was founded in 1936 and opened once again by Mahatma Gandhi. A short distance from the Buddhist temple is an unpretentious church supposedly for low caste Indians who had converted to Christianity. Named St. Thomas' Church, it was designed by Walter George and built in 1932 with red coloured bricks. But, unfortunately, it was in a bad shape till recently and not many people are willing, or have enough money, to restore this unique church.

Jama Masjid of New Delhi.

If we retrace our steps to Gol Dak Khana, right opposite the Cathedral Church of Sacred Heart on Baba Kharak Singh Marg, which was earlier called Irwin Road, stands the sacred Rakab Ganj Sahib. This gurdwara was built on the spot hallowed by the cremation of Guru Teg Bahadur, who was beheaded at the instance of Mughal Emperor Aurangzeb. Sikh military leader, Baghel Singh, who occupied Delhi in 1783, built Rakab Ganj in the same year. Lutyens and his team of New Delhi builders, while surveying the site for New Delhi, are supposed to have reported that this was a Sikh shrine that was impossible to remove.

It is rather surprising that within a short distance from Rakab Ganj there is another gurdwara called Bangla Sahib, near Parliament House. It is called Bangla Sahib because Raja Jai Singh of Jaipur had a bungalow here in the seventeenth century. Guru Har Krishan stayed here in 1664. There is a sacred tank inside and its water is considered extremely holy.

Two important Hindu temples that need mentioning are Hanuman Mandir and Bhairon Mandir. The former, next to the Regal Building on Baba Kharak Singh Marg, was supposed to have been built by Maharajah Man Singh of Amber, during Mughal Emperor Akbar's reign. The other temple, probably the oldest living temple, is located right under the ruined walls of Purana Qila on the eastern side. It is supposed to have been there from the time of the Mahabharata.

As for mosques, it is unfortunate that no important mosque was in existence here till a small one was built after India's Independence, opposite Parliament House.

Making Memories

The summer of 1952 was when I began to work as a photojournalist, clicking Lutyens' Delhi as my subject. Now, sixty years later, as I try to finish this book, on 2 June 2012, I went out to photograph, may be for the last time in my life, certain aspects of New Delhi that I had missed out earlier. In spite of a very hot morning, and my age almost touching eighty,

Aerial view of Connaught Place, 2007.

the clear sunshine helped me to complete my work just before the sun was at its highest point. After Walter George's St. Thomas' Church was captured with my digital camera, I began my drive back home to Faridabad. I could not help but recollect how fortunate I have been in photographing New Delhi for six decades. Though there was a long gap of almost thirty years, bordering almost on neglect, New Delhi had come to my rescue in 1999 when I was in serious trouble.

Three decades earlier, for more than three months in the winter of 1968-1969, I had worked with an American scholar in photographing Lutyens' and Baker's creations in New Delhi. Then, all of a sudden, in spite of our cordial relationship, this young man suddenly disappeared from New Delhi. What was even more distressing was that, in 1982, while visiting my parents in Oxford, I found that he had published a book on New Delhi, and many of the photographs including those on the covers were taken by me in 1969. Yet there was not a single line mentioning my name as one of the photographers. After a bitter acrimony with the publisher and the author, all I got was a tiny printed slip of paper pasted on the photo

The Secretary's bungalow in President's Estate.

credit of that book. After returning to New Delhi from the UK and out of sheer disappointment and frustration, all my New Delhi photographs, negatives, as well as colour slides, went into a cardboard box. I did not open that box for many many years. Then call it fate, destiny or the will of God—all my Delhi photographs, especially those of New Delhi, taken from the early fifties, came to my rescue at a very critical and crisis-ridden period of my life, towards the end of 1999. One day, while discussing some of my tiger photographs for possible covers of books on Jim Corbett, one of the directors of a British publishing house asked if I had some of the old photographs of New Delhi, which he had seen published in many newspapers and magazines long ago. My answer was, "May be both yes and no." Rather puzzled, this gentleman told me that if I could show him those photographs and colour slides within the next three days, there would be a good chance to get some of them accepted and published in a book called *The Millennium Book on New Delhi*.

For the next forty-eight hours, working day and night, I dug out many photographs, negatives and slides and, after getting them printed urgently, I showed them to the publishing house director as well as the commissioning editor. They were overwhelmed to see those vintage photographs and also promised that they would commission me for contemporary photographs of New Delhi, which could range from many of the new hotels and office buildings to traffic conditions and the flora and fauna of New Delhi. Once again, after many years, I put my heart and soul into that assignment and managed to photograph several aspects of New Delhi and the life of its people, which had undergone a dramatic change over a period of more than three decades.

By the time I was given the green signal to go ahead with my assignment, it was almost the last week of the twentieth century. On the very first day of this millennium, when I wanted to start work, there was a setback for outdoor photography—a curtain of dense fog hung all around our flat in Mayur Vihar. Yet, not ready to give up easily, I set out for Lutyens' Delhi with two of my old but trusted single-lens reflex cameras. My first stop was the Taj Mansingh, the first multi-storey hotel to come up in the heart of New Delhi. I wanted to take a few semi-aerial shots from the top of that hotel. However, no one in the front desk, or even a manager, was ready to give me permission to go on the roof or a location on the top floor. The reason given was that one of their lady clients had jumped to her death.

So, after walking out in a huff, I decided to try my luck at the Oberoi Intercontinental (now known as The Oberoi), which had opened in 1965 and, after Imperial Hotel on Janpath, was among the first five star hotels of New Delhi. At this place the staff members were not only courteous but also arranged an escort to accompany me to the roof in practically no time. The view from the top was exactly what I had in mind. Beyond a wide stretch of greenery formed by New Delhi's Golf Club, one could see a conglomeration of high-rise buildings around Connaught Place. Yet, I cannot remember having seen a single one in the early sixties when I was on the same roof while working for SPA. The main Golf Club building appeared like a mock Swiss chalet with its gabled roof and was typical of various styles of architecture frequently seen around New Delhi.

After finishing my work, when I came down to the entrance lounge, I had an opportunity to watch the crowd, all well-heeled men and women showing off their mobile phones, still a novelty on the first day of this twenty-first century. From there the journey to Connaught Place was completed in a plebian Blue Line bus. Sitting next to the driver practically on the engine bonnet, I was soon rewarded with a lucky shot of an entire family of four squeezed on a motor bike, including a baby clinging to the mother. This dangerous problem, still common on New Delhi roads in spite of a strict law, should have been solved long ago by proper planning and the provision of adequate public transport. A little ahead on the same Mathura Road, I had a chance to see another sight, common on Delhi roads. Just ahead of my bus, waiting patiently at a traffic light, was a decorated pachyderm standing among motor vehicles and two-wheelers. As soon as the light turned green, the elephant moved on along with all the other vehicles as if it was used to doing that all its life. New Delhi was probably the only city where the outer Ring Road had a sign saying that elephants were prohibited to walk along the highway.

A traffic jam on a New Delhi road.

At last, after photographing some fast-food joints as well as shopping arcades, which were just not there before the turn of the last century, my assignment for the book was over for the day.

One of the toughest tasks for this book was to photograph the official bungalow of the Secretary to the President. That particular bungalow was designed by A.G. Shoosmith for Private Secretaries to the Viceroys of India. In the early seventies I used to visit that bungalow often as a privileged friend of the late Dr. Ashok Mitra, ICS, who was then the Secretary to the President, V.V. Giri. Unfortunately, I could not locate a single photograph this time and, owing to very stringent rules about security, I had to wait for nearly two weeks before I could complete that task.

Finally, after receiving an invitation to attend the launch of *The Millennium Book on New Delhi*, I entered the President's House once again in late January 2001. The ceremony was held with a lot of fanfare in the Ashoka Hall, which was designed by Lutyens as the main ballroom of British Viceroys and the late President K.R. Narayanan released the book in the presence of the then Prime Minister Atal Behari Vajpayee. This was followed by high tea. I came out of the Ashoka Hall and, after passing through the Durbar Hall, stood next to Emperor Ashoka's stone bull. In front, beyond the lit Jaipur Column and two blocks of Secretariat buildings, was the Central Vista with the floodlit War Memorial Arch, now called the India Gate, gleaming in the distance.

After living in the capital city for more than six decades, various circumstances compelled me to move on to the National Capital Region town of Faridabad in the autumn of 2005. By then I could complete and

New Delhi skyline, 2007.

publish a book on Delhi illustrated with photographs taken by me since 1946. *Delhi: Light, Shades, Shadows* was thanks to the initiative taken by the publisher couple, Bikash and Tultul Niyogi. The reception and sale of this book was well beyond my expectations.

Once again, just after Lutyens' Delhi had completed seventy-five years, I was commissioned to do this book on New Delhi and I wanted to put my newly-acquired digital cameras to good use. I was particularly interested to record the changes that had come about in and around Connaught Place and the once quiet roads such as Curzon Road as well as Barakhamba Road. Both these roads had spacious single- or two-storeyed villas that were residences of industrialists such as Lala Shri Ram, and his sons Charat Ram and Bharat Ram. To record the total transformation that had taken place in these areas with the coming up of high-rise commercial buildings, I decided to visit the revolving restaurant on the top of a high tower just off Connaught Circus.

What was really surprising about the ever-changing panorama from this vantage point was not only a splendid view of Lutyens' Delhi with all its greenery, but also of Old Delhi, including Red Fort, Jama Masjid and the River Yamuna winding across right up to the horizon. Nearby, many high-rise structures such as the eighty-metre-high *Hindustan Times* building, completed in 1973 and Ansal Tower, the first high-rise building to come up in New Delhi, along with the pyramid-shaped New Delhi Municipal Council (NDMC) building, seemed to dwarf the triangular structure of the Samrat Yantra inside Jantar Mantar, once the tallest structure around Connaught Place. The only saving grace of Lutyens' Delhi appeared to be large masses of green trees, planted perhaps by Grierson and Mustoe long ago, which had given a refreshing look to what New Delhi has become today—a concrete jungle.

The last week of November 2011, the date for the completion of a century since the holding of the Delhi Durbar by King George V, was fast approaching and I was feeling rather restless and somewhat sad. Many of my photographs of Delhi as well as New Delhi, taken from the mid-fifties as a young photojournalist, were yet to find a place in any exhibition. All of a sudden, one morning, I received a call and an unknown voice announced that he was Rahaab Allana, the curator of the famous Alkazi Foundation for the Arts.

He said that, on behalf of the Alkazi Foundation, he was organising an exhibition, 'Dawn Upon Delhi', for the National Gallery of Modern Art. He wanted to see my photographs, especially those similar to the ones published in *Delhi: Light, Shades, Shadows*. I searched frantically in my cupboard and was able to dig out a fair number of exhibition prints, which included a few taken by my wife Malabika. Rahaab found them interesting and chose mainly those pictures that showed some unusual and human aspects of the capital city, rather than just its architectural beauty. Thanks to the initiative taken by the National Gallery of Modern

Art and the Ministry of Culture, the exhibition was declared open on 13 February, the date when New Delhi was inaugurated by Lord Irwin in 1931.

On 15 December 2012, I got a chance to enter Rashtrapati Bhavan once again and photograph the Changing of Guards' ceremony before the Jaipur Column. In response to my e-mail request, I had received permission to shoot here. That particular Saturday morning the sky was cloudy and far from being ideal for photography. But taking pictures of the grand spectacle of horse guards galloping past, the march past by guards, as well as the regimental guard band playing familiar marching tunes was a fitting conclusion to my sixty years of association with Rashtrapati Bhavan and the capital city of India, New Delhi.

Changing of Guards' ceremony, Rashtrapati Bhavan, 15 December 2012.